THE SUPERNATURAL
IN SHAKESPEARE.

THE

SUPERNATURAL IN SHAKESPEARE.

By

HELEN HINTON STEWART.

London :

JOHN OUSELEY
16 Farringdon Street
1908.

—

The Supernatural in Shakespeare.

CONTENTS.

THE SUPERNATURAL IN SHAKESPEARE.

I.

PRESENTIMENTS.

There has always been in the human heart a strong desire to peer beyond the boundaries of human existence, and to obtain a glimpse of that mysterious something which, although hidden from the senses, seems to vibrate in harmony with some secret chord within.

From before the day when King Saul of Israel sought help of the Witch of Endor in order to read the future, the supernatural has never ceased to have an attraction for the mass of humanity; and, far from having outgrown this curiosity, we of the present day turn upon it the light of organised inquiry, and give to ghost-lore the dignity of a science.

It is evident that Shakespeare shared this interest with his fellow men in a degree proportioned to his genius. In his plays he introduces us to the awful abode of ghosts, the exquisite world of fairies, the unseen but active sphere of nymphs and sprites, and the weird conclaves of witches with a realism that makes us forget to regard them as mere creatures of the imagination, while they remain, nevertheless, quite distinct from the grosser world of material existence.

Oberon, Titania, Puck, Ariel, and even little Peaseblossom, who does not feel that the realms of the unknown are the richer for these familiar and lovable spirits?

PRESENTIMENTS.

Such apparitions appear only in a limited number of the dramas, but through almost the whole of the Shakespeare plays a subtle breath of metaphysics may be apprehended in the form of dreams and presentiments, and it is in connection with these that I would venture in this paper to suggest a few thoughts.

A presentiment may be superficially defined as an instinctive conviction that something, good or bad as the case may be, is going to happen. This conviction takes possession of the mind without any apparent reason, but there may have been events in the past life or elements in the character of persons concerned that suggest a coming crisis.

In the words of Shakespeare himself :—

3

SUPERNATURAL IN SHAKESPEARE.

" There is a history in all men's lives
  Figuring the nature of the times
    deceased,
  The which observed, a man may
    prophesy
  With a near aim, of the main chance
    of things
  As yet not come to life."

                    (2 *Henry IV.*, III., I.).

Under certain conditions this process
may take place unconsciously within the
brain, resulting in a vague premonition
of coming good or evil, those conditions
being an intellect keen enough to see
below the surface, an imagination capable
of projecting itself into the future, a
temperament, either by nature or force of
circumstances, more introspective than
energetic. Such, in fact, are the attributes
of the persons in Shakespeare who have

the power of anticipating the future.
Under this heading of unconscious cere-
bration must be classed by far the greatest
number of presentiments in the plays.

Hamlet's well-known utterance to
Horatio before his duel with Laertes
readily occurs as an example :—

" Thou would'st not think how ill all's
here about my heart."—(V. 2.).

Hamlet could not guess that Laertes
would use a poisoned dagger. Being
himself the soul of honour, it was the last
idea that would occur to him. But he
knew that he had killed the father of his
proposed antagonist, and that he was
responsible for the madness and death of
his sister, Ophelia. He knew that the
king who had proposed the combat was

his deadly enemy, for he had in his possession at that moment an order, signed by the same king, for his execution in England.

Had Hamlet's character been different, had he been active, energetic, capable of carving out his own future and forcing circumstances to give way before him, this unconscious reasoning would either have passed unnoticed through his brain, or would have led him to grapple with events and avoid the catastrophe. Horatio urges him to act upon the warning :—

" If your mind mislike anything, obey it. I will forstall your repair thither, and say you are not fit."

But it was more consistent with Hamlet's character to "defy augury" than to defy fate, and he walks into the toils prepared for him.

Let us turn to another instance from the play of Richard II., when his unhappy queen moans out :—

" Some unborn sorrow, ripe in fortune's
    womb,
  Is coming towards me, and my inward
    soul
  At nothing trembles."—(II., 2.).

Notwithstanding Richard's vices as a king, which Shakespeare makes clear enough, he is portrayed in the play as a loving husband, and the queen as a devoted wife.

In the garden scene, where with her ladies, she observes the two gardeners in close conclave, she shows keen intelligence in her sad wager.—

7

" My wretchedness unto a row of pins
  They'll talk of State; for every one
      doth so
Against a change."—(III., 4.).

Her sweet imagination pours itself
forth as King Richard approaches,
dethroned and guarded :—

" But soft, but see, or rather do not see
My fair rose wither; yet look up behold,
That you in pity may dissolve to dew
And wash him fresh again."—(V., 1.).

And thus, although all seemed well
when Richard, still in the full tide of
power and fortune, bids her farewell and
starts for Ireland to quell the rebellion
there, it is not strange that "her inmost
soul" should "grieve at something more
than parting from my lord the king."
She must have read the discontent beneath

8

the cold and ceremonious respect of the old nobility, the selfish greed hidden under the flattery of Bushey, Green, and others, the seething unrest of the country at large, increased by the last and greatest injustice to the heir of the popular Duke of Lancaster. But it was only a sensation, not a consciously reasoned conviction, and thus she could say with truth :—

" Nothing hath begot my something grief,
    Or something hath the nothing that I grieve ;
    'Tis in reversion that I do possess."—
    (II., 2.).

The next presentiment to be considered comes from the lips of Juliet, a creature brimming over with intellect, and poetry,

9

and fire—Juliet, who, from an irresponsible, obedient child of fourteen, was
transformed in one day into the most
courageous, the most constant, and the
most firm of all the women of that
wonderful world which Shakespeare has
created.

> " Although I joy in thee,
> I have no joy of this contract to-night,
> It is too rash, too unadvised, too
> sudden."—(II., 2.).

She is in the first flush of her love for
Romeo, and she knows that it is returned; although she is aware of the
enmity between the houses of Capulet
and Montagu, she might naturally, with
the Friar, look forward to a period of
sweet, secret love and ultimate reconciliation between the rival families. But

PRESENTIMENTS.

Juliet's high-strung, imaginative nature looks deeper. The dogmatic father, the unsympathetic mother, the passionate and arrogant cousins, the very intensity of her own emotions create an atmosphere in her mind that, with a sudden pang, suggests the possibility of some dark catastrophe. Throughout the play one is haunted with the feeling of the inevitable. It is true that if the Friar had come a little sooner to the tomb, if Juliet had awakened from her sleep a little earlier, the dénouement might have been different, but we are made to feel from the first that nothing but the death of the two unhappy victims of its bitterness could have put an end to the passionate feud.

We now turn to Calphurnia, who, on

11

the night before the "Ides of March," dreamt that Cæsar's statue spouted blood, and thrice cried out in her sleep, "Help, ho, they murder Cæsar." Had she also the union of intellect and imagination necessary to forecast the future?

There is not much to interest us in Cæsar's wife; her general manner is a combination of impulsiveness and wifely duty; but one remark betrays deeper intuition than on the surface appeared. After Cæsar's hyperbolical vaunt:—

" Danger knows full well
That Cæsar is more dangerous than he;
We are two lions littered in one day,
And I the elder and more terrible."—
    (II., 2.);

PRESENTIMENTS.

Calphurnia answers quickly :—

> " Alas, my lord,
> Your wisdom is consumed in con-
> fidence."
> Then she at once reverts to her
> womanly pleadings :—
> " Do not go forth to-day.   Call it my
> fear
> That keeps you in the house, and not
> your own."

The criticism is too just to have been
conceived on the spur of the moment.
It is evident that she was able to gauge
the hero's weakness, and see the rock on
which he was likely to split.   Nor is
she wanting in the gift of imagination, as
is proved by her summing up of
a poetical thought in words that have
become proverbial :—

" When beggars die there are no comets
    seen ;
The heavens themselves blaze forth
    the death of princes."

Had she been more free, her energy
might have overcome the tendency to
introspection, but, as Cæsar's wife, she
could but dream and entreat.

The apparition of Cæsar's ghost to
Brutus, forewarning him of his death ;
Cassius' pessimistic interpretation of the
appearance above his army of the
"ravens, crows, and kites"; Shylock's
charge :—

      "Jessica, my girl,
Look to my house—I am right loath
    to go,
There is some ill abrewing towards
    my rest,
For I did dream of money-bags to-
    night,"—(II., 5.) ;

all come under the same category and need not be further discussed here.

Instinctive anticipations of good fortune are much less frequent in the plays. Helena, in "All's Well That Ends Well," provides us with one instance, and with it we must close the first class of Shakespearean presentiments.

Helena has in her possession some specific remedies bequeathed to her by her father, a learned physician. Among them is a cure for the disease under which the king is suffering, and Helena determines to set out for Paris to see the king —more, however, in the hope of winning young Bertram for a husband than out of pity for the royal sufferer. In addition to her faith in the nostrum, she has an inner conviction that she will be able to

15

overcome all hindrances, and that her
efforts will be crowned with success—a
pleasant presentiment which she expresses as follows :—

> " There's something in't
> More than my father's skill, which
>   was the greatest
> Of his profession, that his good receipt
> Shall for my legacy be sanctified
> By the luckiest stars or heaven."
>
> (I. 3.).

The result justified her optimism, and
her optimism was probably the result of
the consciousness of her own strength of
purpose, and an inner knowledge of the
characters with whom she has to deal.
Her intellect requires no comment, and
the periphrases by which she expresses
what a modern doctor would describe as

"forty-eight hours," speaks volumes
for her imagination.

" Ere twice the horses of the sun shall
    bring
  Their fiery torches his diurnal ring;
  Ere twice in murk and occidental
    damp
  Moist Hesperus hath quenched his
    sleepy lamp," &c.—(II., 1.).

The softer side of her fancy appears in
such expressions as the following :—

        " 'Twere all one
  That I should love a bright, particular
    star,
  And seek to wed it, he is so above me."
                                 (I. 1.).

" I know I love in vain, strive against
    hope;
  Yet in this captious and intenable
    sieve,
  I still pour in the waters of my love."
                                 (I. 3.).

B

PRESENTIMENTS.

II.

Shakespeare does not confine the occult gift to individuals. The mass of the people are also susceptible to the signs of the times, and see, sometimes in the phenomena of Nature sometimes in their own hearts, prophetic warning of evils to come.

In Richard III., Act II., Scene 3, the dramatist gives us at once an example and a definition of this.—

" 2ND CITIZEN : Truly the souls of men
are full of dread :
Ye cannot reason al-
most with a man
That looks not heavily
and full of fear.

18

PRESENTIMENTS.

" 3RD CITIZEN : By a divine instinct
men's minds mistrust
Ensuing dangers, as by
proof we see
The waters swell before
a boisterous storm."

It is interesting to note in passing that
the "proof" in this instance is founded
on an error of fact, an error shared by
his contemporary, Francis Bacon, who
writes in his Essay of Sedition :—"As
there are certain hollow blasts of wind
and secret swelling of sea before a
tempest, so there are in States."
This, however, does not affect the
statement that human instinct foresees
national trouble.   As animal instinct is
developed and modified by environment,
so the divine instinct in man evolves out

19

of the combined intellect and imagination of the mass, guided by current events and the influence of prominent characters.

In "Julius Cæsar" we have also examples of presentiment of evil among the people, but in a more objective form. Prodigies are seen or imagined, and ordinary sounds and sights are interpreted as evil omens.

Before Cæsar's assassination we hear that :—

" A lioness hath whelped in the streets;
    And graves have yawned and yielded
        up their dead;
    Fierce fiery warriors fought upon the
        clouds
    In rank and squadrons and right forms
        of war," etc.

In the play of "King John," Hubert tells the guilty monarch :—

20

PRESENTIMENTS.

" They say five moons were seen to-
    night,
Four fixed, and the fifth did whirl
    about
The other four in wondrous motion . .
Old men and beldams in the street
Do prophesy about it dangerously."

The third class of occult experience to
which Shakespeare introduces us in his
plays may be termed ironical presentiment :—

" Before ill chances men are ever merry,
But heaviness foreruns the good
    event."

This mental attitude is the reverse of
that which we have been discussing, and
accordingly we find it exhibited in very
different characters. Those characters
are not without imagination, but it is

unbalanced by reason. They project themselves into the future as in the former two classes, but without a mental grasp of the circumstances; or it may be that their reason is blinded by some false estimate of themselves or of others concerned.

Thus it was with the powers of France before the battle of Agincourt :—

"Will it never be day!" cries the Dauphin. "I will trot to-morrow a mile, and my way will be paved with English faces."

"Who will go hazard with me for twenty prisoners?" demands Ramillies; and the constable of France echoes :—

"Would it were day! Alas, poor Harry of England! He longs not for the dawning as we do!"—(*Henry V.,* III., 7.).

But the ill chance follows soon upon, and as the natural consequence of this over-confident merriment, and the Dauphin, appreciating, after the battle, the irony of events, exclaims :—

" Reproach and everlasting shame,
  Sits mocking in our plumes."

(IV.5.).

In the great Scottish tragedy we find Hecuba, the queen of the witches, laying herself out to produce this state of mind in Macbeth. By the aid of potent spells and deceptive prophecies she arouses in him

"Such artificial sprites (spirits)
  As by the strength of their illusion

23

Shall draw him on to his confusion :
He shall spurn fate, scorn death, and
  bear
 His hopes 'bove wisdom, grace, or
  fear :
And you all know security
Is mortal's chiefest enemy."—(III. 5.).

Accordingly we see Macbeth fighting
with undaunted bravery, until this
borrowed courage is staggered by the
apparent approach of Dunsinane Wood,
and changed to desperation when he
learns that Macduff was "untimely
ripped from his mother's womb." It is
only by a stretch of terms, however,
that his grim optimism can be described
as "merriment."

Turning to the play "2 Henry IV.,"
we find the rebels under Mowbray, the
Archbishop, and Hastings in parley with

24

PRESENTIMENTS.

Prince John of Lancaster, Westmoreland, and others of the King's officers.

The Prince having received articles, or conditions, of surrender, from the malcontents, promises to redress the grievances, charges them thereupon to "discharge your forces as we will ours," and invites them to "drink together friendly and embrace." The Archbishop and Hastings, who have argued themselves into a conviction that peace is more to the advantage of the King than the continuance of civil war, accept the proposal joyfully, but Mowbray, with truer instinct, regards it with distrust. The following conversation ensues :—

"ARCH. To you, my noble Lord of
Westmoreland,

25

WEST. I pledge your grace; and if
you knew what pains
I have bestowed to breed this
present peace,
You would drink freely; but
my love to you
Shall show itself more openly
hereafter.

ARCH. I do not doubt it.

WEST.　　　I am glad of it.
Health to my lord and gentle
cousin, Mowbray.

MOW. You wish me health in very
happy season,
For I am on a sudden something ill.

ARCH. Against ill chances men are
ever merry
But heaviness foreruns the
good event.

WEST. Therefore be merry, coz;
since sudden sorrow
Serves to say this: some

26

good thing comes to-
morrow.

ARCH. Believe me, I am passing
light in spirit.

Mow. So much the worse if your
own rule be true."—(II. 2.)

Readers of the play know that the rebel
army, on receiving from Hastings the
order to disperse, joyfully "take their
courses east, west, north, south"; but the
Prince's soldiers, having received charge
from their commander to "stand," refuse
to move at the command of Westmoreland, "until they hear the Prince's
voice." Helpless without their soldiers,
the Archbishop and Hastings are startled
from their fool's paradise to find themselves arrested as traitors.

Another instance of high spirits

preceding disaster may be found in the comedy of "Love's Labour's Lost."

Merriment is at its height among the ladies of the Princess of France and their royal mistress. Their host, the King of Navarre, and his lords have been cheated and mocked, the rustics who had prepared a performance for their amusement have been "flouted out of their parts," Don Armado and Costard, egged on by the nobles, are on the point of fighting a ridiculous duel, when Mercades enters with the greeting :—

" God save you, Madam."

" Welcome, Mercades," cries the laughing Princess, " but that thou interruptest our merriment."

" I am sorry, madam, for the news I
bring

Is heavy on my tongue. The King,
　　your father—"
" Dead, for my life!" escapes from the
paralysed lips of the royal lady.

The sudden revulsion of feeling seems
to have suggested the worst that could
befall, and made her a true prophetess.
　There is nothing to connect this light-
hearted conduct with the death of the
King, except the coincidence of the time,
but it is evident from the last scene of the
play that the Princess and the Lady
Rosaline are impressed with the danger
and unseemliness of too complete an
abandonment to mirth.
　There are a few instances of presentiments in the plays still un-
accounted for. They might perhaps be
defined as a group of exceptions, save

29

that they have this in common, that there is nothing to account for the pre-sentiment unless it be what we should now call thought-vibration. That this idea was not a stranger to Shakespeare—as what idea of any beauty or value was?—we see from Imogen's regret that she had not had time to charge her banished husband :—

" At the sixth hour of morn, at noon, at midnight
  To *encounter me* with orisons, for then
  I am in heaven for him."
            (*Cymbeline*, I. 3.).

We find the first example in "Much Ado About Nothing," when Hero, in the act of choosing and donning her wedding dress sighs out :—

PRESENTIMENTS.

" God give me joy to wear it, for my
heart is exceeding heavy."

Till that moment there has been
nothing to suggest a melancholy disposition in Hero. She is quieter than
her cousin, but has plenty of spirit. She
has been wooed and won by young
Claudio. She has entered heartily into
the plot of hoaxing Beatrice and Benedict
into a belief that each is dying for love
of the other. And now the wedding-day
has arrived without any hitch that she
knows of.

But, during the night that has just
passed, a treacherous plot has been
carried out against her peace and honour.
At the moment she is speaking the con-
stables and watchmen are bursting with
the importance of their discovery,

31

Borachio is brooding over his guilt, and Claudio and Don Pedro have their minds full of their intention of insulting and denouncing the innocent bride at the very alter. There is nothing, and has been nothing, to give Hero any clue to this, except that mysterious preception of the inner spirit for which we have not yet found a name sufficiently subtle.

Again in "Troilus and Cressida" we can trace no series of events to account for the passionate excitement of Cassandra and Hecuba and Andromache when Hector is about to issue, for the last time, as it proves to be, from the walls of Troy to do battle with the Greeks.

He had done so many times before and returned loaded with honour. The previous day he had met Ajax in single

32

combat, but recognising in him his "father's sister's son," he declines to fight more, a truce is proclaimed, and Hector is feasted in the tents of Agamemnon and Achilles.

And yet Andromache had dreamed of "bloody turbulence, and this whole night hath nothing been but shapes and forms of slaughter." Even old Priam urges :—

" Thy wife hath dreamed, thy mother
    hath had visions :
  Cassandra doth foresee, and I myself
  Am like a prophet suddenly enrapt
  To tell thee that this day is ominous."
                              (V. 3.).

But the dramatist has already made us aware that Achilles' hatred and jealousy of Hector had been increased tenfold by the meeting of the rival heroes, that he

c

was planning in his tent to meet Hector "fell as death" upon the field, and that in the depth of his heart he was determined, if fair fight could not accomplish his hated rival's defeat, to call treachery to his aid.

And lastly we have the dream of the lover, Romeo, on the night preceding the climax of his tragic career.

Banished from Verona, far from his beloved wife of a day, with the blood of Tybalt upon his conscience, he awoke in the morning with a strange sense of happiness :—

" If I may trust the flattering truth of
    sleep
  My dreams presage some joyful news at
    hand;
  My bosom's lord sits lightly on its
    throne;

PRESENTIMENTS.

And all this day an unaccustomed
    spirit
Lifts me above the ground with
    cheerful thoughts," &c.—(V. 1.).

And at that moment Balthazar enters with
the news that Juliet is dead.

Our first impulse might be to place
this episode in the third group as a case
of mirth before ill-chance; but on closer
study we are more inclined to see in it
sympathetic thought-reading between the
lovers, and to exclaim: Oh, if only
Romeo had trusted this faithful instinct!
If he had only kept up his courage and
his hope.

For Juliet was not dead. At the time
when he was happy in dreamland she
had proved herself capable of the loftiest
devotion, and was now lying, in a trance,

35

indeed, and in the abode of death, but alive and well; the plans were all complete, and that very day the husband and wife might have been together in Mantua, the town of his adoption, waiting until the Friar, having brought about a reconciliation between the respective parents, recalled them to Verona.

But only the brief vision vouchsafed to Romeo in the night and the Friar's rehearsal of his defeated plans over the dead bodies of the lovers, remain to tell us what might have been. Apart from historical or legendary fact, it was more dramatically true that it should be so. The tragic elements surrounding the unhappy pair were too strong, their Southern blood was too impulsive for the stream of life to flow smoothly, and the tale moves on, though through apparent accident, to its inevitable conclusion.

If we turn, as in the first three classes, to the author himself to find some words by which to define this last group of presentiments, we think irresistibly of Hamlet's well-known utterance, the truth of which is becoming more apparent every day :—

" There are more things in heaven and
    earth, Horatio,
Than are dreamt of in our philosophy."
                (I., 5.).

PART II.

—

GHOSTS.

I.

Shakespeare introduces us in all to fourteen visitants from another world, eleven of whom appear in one play. Of the other three each has a whole drama for its environment. It is impossible to be certain from a perusal of the plays whether the author himself believed in the apparitions he created, but, when we consider the state of philosophy and of religion in those days, it is highly probable that he did.

Bacon, the greatest philosopher of the age, looked upon spirits, both good and bad, as a legitimate subject of study. "So of degenerate and revolted spirits," he writes in "Advancement of Learning,"

38

book ii., "the conversing with them or the employment of them is prohibited, much more any veneration towards them. But the contemplation or science of their nature, their power, their illusions, either by Scripture or reason is part of spiritual wisdom. For so the apostle saith, 'We are not ignorant of his stratagems.'

And it is no more unlawful to inquire the nature of evil spirits than to inquire the force of poison in nature, or the nature of sin and vice in morality." It would have been interesting if Bacon had given us the result of his study of evil spirits, but he only notes that much has already been written on the subject, for the most part "too fabulous and fantastical." In the same book, however, when treating of the imagination, he asserts that the

power of divining the future (which may
be held to include seeing visions) is
greatest when "the mind is withdrawn
and collected into itself, and not diffused
into the organs of the body; which ap-
peareth most in sleep, in ecstasies, and
near death."

With this clue to the ghost-lore of the
period, we may proceed to consider the
treatment of the subject in the plays,
opining that the poet is not less credulous
nor, perhaps, less scientific than the philosopher.

From a chronological point of view
the ghost of Hamlet's father claims our
first attention. The play of "Hamlet" is
alluded to in contemporary literature in
1589, and other references show that it
was known on the stage as early as 1586.

GHOSTS.

It was published in its original form in 1603; and although it was reprinted in 1604, "revised and enlarged to nearly as much again," having assumed the magnificent form in which we now know it, the Ghost has undergone little or no modification.

The foundation of the story is taken from "Saxo Grammaticus," and from the "Histoires Tragiques of Belleforest," but the Ghost is the author's own invention, and bears every mark of being the creation of a youthful genius. This well-known apparition occupies an unique position among the supernatural visitants of the plays, in that it defies all attempt at scientific explanation. There is neither sleep, nor ecstasy, nor the approach of death, nor disordered imagination to account for its appearance to Marcellus and Bernardo and Horatio; and when the Queen, on the occasion of its second appearance to Hamlet, exclaims :—

" This is the very coinage of your brain.
This bodiless creation ecstasy
Is very cunning in,"

Hamlet repudiates it at once :

"Ecstasy !
My pulse as yours does temperately keep time,
And makes as healthful music . . .
Mother, for love of grace
Lay not a flattering unction to your soul
That not your trespass, but my madness speaks."

And the reader is made to feel with him that such sophistry cannot explain the case.

42

GHOSTS.

The Ghost has the power of making himself visible to whom he will, and perseveres in his visits to the watchers on the lonely ramparts till he has attained his purpose of speaking to young Hamlet. To him he confides that he has come direct from purgatory, where, ostensibly because he had been sent to his account without time to be "aneled," he was

" Doomed for a certain term to walk the
     night,
  And for the day confined to fast in fires,
  Till the foul crimes done in my days
     of nature
  Are burnt and purged away."

He hints at the horrors of his place of abode (happily for the theology of the time a temporary one !), gives a detailed account of the method of his murder, even to the working of the poison in his system, and urges revenge. When compelled by the crowing of the cock to return to his "prison-house," he makes his voice audible, in his descent, from beneath the ground.

Throughout we are reminded, on the one hand, of the arbitrary appearances of the gods in the Greek drama, and on the other, of the crudest teaching of the Catholic Church. Various superstitions are glanced at, besides the one he so beautifully describes, in the words of Marcellus :—

" Some say that ever 'gainst the season comes,
Wherein our Saviour's birth is celebrated,

44

GHOSTS.

The bird of dawning singeth all night
    long;
And then, they say, no spirit dare stir
    abroad,
The nights are wholesome, then no
    planets strike,
No fairy takes, nor witch hath power to
    charm,
So hallowed and so gracious is the
    time."

Horatio suggests an idea which is at
the root of some of the most blood-
curdling of our modern ghost stories
when he says to Hamlet :—

" What if it tempt you toward the flood,
    my lord,
Or to the dreadful summit of the cliff
That beetles o'er its base into the sea,
And there assume some other horrible
    form

45

That might deprive your sovereignty
of reason
And draw you into madness."

When Hamlet, later in the play, is
meditating on the appearance and the
message of the Ghost, he gives utterance
to a thought which is as old as Euri-
pedes :—

"The spirit that I have seen
May be the devil : and the devil hath
power
To assume a pleasing shape; yea, and
perhaps
Out of my weakness and my melancholy,
As he is every potent with such spirits,
Abuses me to damn me."

To Dr. Churton Collins we are indebted
for the information that in the tragedy of
"Electra" Orestes expresses exactly the
same doubt under very similar circum-

stances : "But was it not some demon in the likeness of a god enjoined it ?" (i.e., the revenge for the murder by his mother, Clytemnestra, of his father, Agamemnon). We are also reminded of Bacon's suggestive quotation in reference to the chief of evil spirits, "For we are not ignorant of his stratagems."

In the various editions of the play, even up till the folio of 1623, no essential difference is made, as has been said, in the character of the Ghost, utterly different as the whole conception of it is from the other visions of a similar kind. It fitted the time and the subject, and would not appear impossible to the audience. So grand is the general effect that even in our own day we view the disembodied spirit as an integral part of the play.

47

Hamlet with the Ghost left out would be an anomaly second only to the omission of the hero himself.

In the play of "Richard III." we follow that king's career of guilt through the first four acts. Before the opening scene he had already joined in the murder of the young prince, Edward of Lancaster, and slain the mild Sixth Henry with his own hand.

Fortune herself seemed to favour him in the early death of his brother, Edward IV., but he made haste to anticipate the event by clearing his brother Clarence from his path. The son and brother of the widowed queen, with Sir Thomas Vaughan, were next sent to the block on a pretended charge of treason, and were soon followed by the too loyal Hastings.

But the dastardly crime the latter had refused to share in was carried out by other tools of Richard, now crowned king, and the brave young sons of Edward IV. were, by his order, smothered in the tower.

Even now the bloody record was not complete. His own queen was hastened to her doom to make way for a more convenient bride, and, lastly, the Duke of Buckingham, who had helped him to the throne, was sent to execution without even the semblance of a trial.

In the fifth act we see his sins recoiling on his head. A rival claimant crosses the Channel to seize the throne, and many of his nobles forsake his standard to join Henry of Richmond. Then the crisis comes!

On the eve of the decisive battle, as the guilty monarch tries to snatch a few hours of repose, one by one, or in groups of two or three as they suffered, and in exact chronological order, the spirits of his victims pass before him.

There is something appalling in the thought of the active, daring, conscience-less man, tied to his couch by the chains of slumber, helpless to shake off the terrible memories, compelled to act over again each crime, to see the very form of each sufferer, ghastly, reproachful, threat-ening. Awake he would have defied them with some new crime or violent action, but asleep he was at their mercy—he could only gaze and melt in the agony of fear. Although the actual words vary, all address him in the same strain :—

"Despair and die!"

Two of the apparitions makē use of the identical couplet :—

"To-morrow in the battle think of me,
And fall thy edgeless sword, despair
and die !"

They are the brother of his youthful confidence and the wife of his bosom. These two, more than all the others, were able at this crisis of his career when everything depended on decision and courage, to blunt the edge of his weapon.

How true it is to the inner life of humanity that each spirit as it leaves the murderer's tent should breathe into the ear of his dreaming rival words of encouragement and hope, thus filling him not only with confidence in his own

51

D 2

prowess, but with the strengthening conviction that he is working out the will of the Almighty, and that the invisible powers, as well as his visible army, will fight on his behalf. Mark the contrast :—

KING RICHARD: "Give me another horse! bind up my wounds!
Have mercy, Jesu! Soft! I did but dream,
O coward conscience, how dost thou afflict me?
The lights burn blue. It is now dead midnight.
Cold fearful drops stand on my shaking flesh.

. . . . .

I shall despair! there is no creature loves me!
And if I die, no soul shall pity me.
Methought the souls of all that I had murdered

Came to my tent, and every one did
    threat
To-morrow's vengeance on the head of
    Richard.''
RICHMOND : ''The sweetest sleep and
    fairest boding dreams,
That ever entered in a drowsy head
Have I, since your departure had, my
    lords.
Methought their souls, whose bodies
    Richard murdered,
Came to my tent and cried on victory.

    .   .   .   .   .

God and our good cause fight upon our
    side,
The prayers of holy saints and wronged
    souls,
Like high-reared bulwarks, stand before
    our faces.''

Was this experience merely a dream,
or, since ''dreams'' themselves still wait
for elucidation, was it the effect solely of

53

imagination conjuring up the past? The
episode is treated in such a way that it
might be so. Richard, as we know from
his unhappy wife, was subject to bad
dreams, of which this might be but the
climax; all the events of the play lead
up to it, and the spirits appear only to
the two men whose thoughts and interests
are worked to a point, and who await a
crisis of tremendous importance on the
morrow.

But on the other hand, we know that in
Shakespeare's time the highest philosophy admitted, not only the existence of
good and evil spirits, but their illusions,
stratagems, power over mortals, and the
possibility of inquiring into and obtain-
ing some knowledge of their nature.
We have seen, too, that sleep was looked

upon as a medium by which the mind of man came into touch with the unseen world, and saw to some extent into the future.

It seems probable, then, that by the author and audience alike the ghosts, as they passed over the stage might be, and probably were, regarded as the authentic spirits of the departed, predicting with authority the event of the battle, the minds of the sleepers being for the time a part of the unseen world.

Such a belief, and as we have seen the most highly educated of the day might share it with the most ignorant, must have enhanced the effect of the scene to a degree which it is difficult for us in our prosaic age to realise.

GHOSTS.

II.

In "Macbeth" and "Julius Cæsar," as in "Richard III.," the ghost episodes stand on a strictly scientific basis. There is nothing arbitrary in the appearances; whether regarded as psychological phenomena or mental hallucinations, the conditions fulfil every condition of science.

In the case of Macbeth, the oppression of a guilty and still sensitive conscience, and the ecstatic or highly concentrated state of his mind, are enough to account for the vision, real or imaginary, of his victim.

With regard to Brutus, although there is no abnormal excitement, the continu-

ous compelling thought of the dead
Cæsar, intensified by the imminence of
his own death, brings him by degrees
into closer touch with the spiritual atmosphere than with the material world itself.

The Scottish tragedy lies under the
spell of storm and witchcraft as well as
of crime, and the mind of the reader or
spectator is thus fully prepared for the
climax in Act III., where, through the
ghost, Macbeth's conscience makes one
final fruitless effort, then leaves him to
continue his downward career unchecked.

Some time has elapsed since the
murder of Duncan. The murderer and
his no less guilty wife have been duly
crowned, one son of the slaughtered king
has reached Ireland and the other is safe
at the English court. The lords, all save

57

M'Duff, have sworn fealty to Macbeth;
even Banquo, although convinced of the
usurper's guilt, has become, outwardly at
least, his friend and counsellor. But
Macbeth fears Banquo, for

> " In his royalty of nature
> Reigns that which would be feared :
> 'tis much he dares
> And, to that dauntless temper of his
> mind,
> He hath a wisdom that doth guide his
> valour
> To act in safety. There is none but he
> Whose being I do fear : and under him
> My *genius* is rebuked, as it is said
> Mark Antony's was by Cæsar."

In these last words we have the idea
skilfully suggested of the twofold nature
of man. Apart from and, to a certain extent, independent of his material body,

there is the "genius" or immortal spirit. The thought is amplified in "Antony and Cleopatra," II., 3, when the soothsayer, referring to Octavius Cæsar, and speaking to Antony, says :—

" Therefore, O Antony, stay not by his
    side.
  Thy *demon*, that's thy *spirit* that keeps
    thee, is
  Noble, courageous, high, unmatchable,
  Where Cæsar's is not; but near him
    thy *angel*
  Becomes a fear, as being overpowered.

. . . .
    I say again, thy *spirit*
  Is all afraid to govern thee near him;
  But he away, 'tis noble."

The words genius and demon (in their original classic sense of over-soul), angel and spirit are used variously to express this mysterious part of our being, each individual word adding something of its own to the idea to be conveyed.

It was the self-control, the calm restraint of the' young Octavius which "rebuked" the passionate "genius" of the man who would give away a kingdom for an hour's enjoyment. Macbeth's valour, on the other hand, was paralysed by that "royalty of nature" which could dare anything, except to do a mean action, and it was only, as Macbeth knew too well, through a succession of meannesses that he could uphold the position he had so meanly won. While Banquo lived the sword of Damocles hung by its single silken thread above the blood-stained king, as he tried in vain to enjoy life's royal feast.

But now (to use his own metaphor), he has determined to "kill" the "snake" of danger and opposition which so far he had but "scotched," and to be free, once and for all, from fear and suspicion. He forgot, as such men do, that Banquo's body might die, and rot, and return to dust, and yet the *spirit* still live to re-buke, as heretofore, his guilty soul.

In Act III., 2, he betrays in his words to Lady Macbeth the strained and un-settled state of his mind, thus preparing the way still further for the abnormal scene which is to follow :—

MACBETH : "But let the frame of things
   disjoint, both the worlds suffer
  Ere we will eat one meal in fear, and
   sleep
  In the affliction of those terrible dreams

That shake us nightly; better be with
    the dead
Whom we, to gain our peace, have sent
    to peace,
*Than on the torture of the mind to lie
In restless ecstasy."*

And he goes on to hint at his guilty
plot, telling his wife that that night

" There shall be done
A deed of dreadful note."

But when she asks, "What's to be
done?" he answers :—

" Be innocent of the knowledge, dearest
    chuck,
Till thou applaud the deed."

Banquo has ridden forth with his son
Fleance, under promise to return in time
for the evening feast. At one point on

their homeward journey they will dis-
mount, "so all men do," and, leaving
their horses "to go a mile about," will
"walk from hence to reach the palace
gate." Here the deed is to be done.

The guests have assembled and Macbeth mechanically welcomes 'them, but
his mind is full of the crime that is even
then being perpetrated. Through the
windows he sees the last streak of day
disappear from the west and the sky
darken under the heavy clouds that
show

"There will be rain to-night."

The torches cast a ruddy glare over the
loaded table, on the jewels of the Queen
and the scabbards of the nobles, but
throw the far corners of the hall and the

63

doors and recesses in the massive walls into deeper gloom.

Macbeth, leaving the Queen to "keep her state," and himself professing to "play the humble host," passes slowly down the room, exchanges greetings with his nobles, indicates a chair where he will sit, promises presently to "drink a measure," and so makes his way towards the door where his watchful eye has recognised the furtive figure of the hired assassin. On a nearer view he shrinks, for he "still but young in deed," exclaiming :—

"There's blood upon thy face!"

"'Tis Banquo's then,"

answers the murderer, and with grim jest Macbeth responds :—

64

GHOSTS.

" 'Tis better thee without than him
  within."

Then in fearful whispers he learns that
his enemy lies deep in a ditch "with
twenty trenched gashes on his head, each
one a death to nature," but Fleance has
escaped.   Still "cabined, cribbed, confined, bound in to saucy doubts and
fears," but relieved that at least Banquo
for ever silent, Macbeth returns to his
guests and bids them eat with appetite.
With daring braggadocio he even regrets
the absence of the murdered man, and
hopes that unkindness rather than mis-
chance is the cause; then, turning to seat
himself, he finds that Banquo occupies
the empty chair. He has had a glimpse
of the silent figure before, making him
think the table full, but now he sees and

65

E

recognises the bleeding form of his victim.

Macbeth's first words :—

" Which of you have done this ?"

seem to imply that he mistook the appearance for Banquo in the flesh, and made an instinctive effort to divert suspicion from himself.   But a second glance shows him the truth, and he continues, his fascinated eyes returning the stony glare :—

" Thou can'st not say I did it !   Never shake
Thy gory locks at me."

Lady Macbeth hastens to come between his self-betrayal and the astonished nobles, apologising for him, and ending

66

with the contemptuous angry aside to her
husband :—

"Are you a man?"

But Macbeth is oblivious of his guests,
nothing exists for him except that awful
figure as he answers :—

"Yes, and a bold one, that dare look on
    that
Which might appal the devil."

Lady Macbeth perseveres in her whis-
pered remonstrance :—

                    "Oh proper stuff!
This is the very painting of your fear,
This is the air-drawn dagger that you
    said
Led you to Duncan," &c.

Macbeth only answers :—

"Prithee see there! behold! look! lo!
how say you?
Why, what care I? If thou can'st
nod, speak too!
If charnel-houses and our graves must
send
Those that we bury back, our
monuments
Shall be the maws of kites."

The tension is slackening and the spirit
becomes invisible, but his mind has not
as yet sufficiently recovered from its state
of ecstasy to grasp the actual circumstances, and he goes on reasoning with
his own guilty thoughts:—

"Blood hath been shed ere now in the
olden time,
Ere humane statute purged the gentle
weal,
Ay, and since too, murders have been
performed

68

Too terrible for the ear. The time
  hath been
When that the brains were out the man
  would die,
And there an end, but now they rise
  again,
With twenty mortal murders on their
  crown,
And push us from our stools. This
  is more strange
Than such a murder is."

He is coming to himself, and Lady
Macbeth addresses him in conventional
tones :—

            " My worthy lord,
Your noble friends do lack you."

Macbeth is now fully recalled from his
absorption, and speaks to his guests in
hospitable language; but again his
bravado carries him too far :—

"I drink to the general joy of the whole
   table,
   And to our dear friend Banquo, whom
   we miss,
   Would he were here!"

The name is enough, his mind is
caught again in the trance, Banquo is
before him, and everything else is
oblivion.

"Avaunt and quit my sight! Let the
   earth hide thee!
   Thy bones are marrowless, thy blood
   is cold,
   Thou hast no speculation in those eyes
   Which thou dost glare with."

The Queen again intervenes, but Macbeth, all unheeding, challenges the ghost
to appear in any mortal form, however
terrible, and concludes :—

"Hence, horrible shadow!
Unreal mockery, hence!"

It is over, and the spirit disappears.
But the "mirth has been displaced," and
Lady Macbeth hurriedly dismisses the
too curious guests.

Was the ghost, in the meaning of the
poet, a mere shadow and a mockery?
If it had been, it could only have existed
in Macbeth's eye, whereas we know that
it entered some time before Macbeth was
aware of it. This stage-direction, "Enter
Ghost of Banquo and sits in Macbeth's
chair," occurs in the first folio as well as
in the modern editions, and is therefore
a part of the dramatist's purpose. It is
generally urged that Macbeth's mind
had been worked up to a state of abnormal excitement, when the eyes,

71

according to modern recognised science, would be subject to deception, seeing in imagination what was vividly pictured on the brain.

But is it not more likely that, in accordance with the science of his day and of some psychologists of our own, Shakespeare intended to indicate that the concentration or "ecstasy"of Macbeth's mind enabled him to see the spirit of Banquo, that spirit being really present, though invisible to others. Its realistic appearance with gory head and glaring eyes is no objection to this view, as, being bodiless, though a reality, while it made its actual presence *felt* by Macbeth it could only present itself to his *sight* in the form existing in his mind.

For hours afterwards not only the

guilty King, but the Queen also, felt that awful presence in the deserted hall. He mutters at broken intervals that "blood will have blood," that "stones have been known to move," that "maggot-pies and choughs and rooks" have "brought forth the secret'st blood of man," till at last, when night is "at odds with morning which is which," he rouses himself from the spell of fear to plan his culminating act of villainy, the massacre of the wife and children of M'Duff.

GHOSTS.

III.

The Ghost of Cæsar seems at first sight to be of less importance than any other of Shakespeare's apparitions. It has little to say, and remains visible for a very short time. It is seen by none but Brutus, and creates no outward sensation. But when we examine the subject more closely, we find that this vision is a most powerful element in the drama, giving to it a unity of purpose and design which would otherwise be lacking.

It has been often remarked that Brutus, and not Cæsar, is the true hero of the play. This may be so, and in no other hero, perhaps, do we see reflected so much of the character and opinions of the

74

author; but from first to last the spirit of Julius Cæsar is the vital principle of the tragedy.

"O Julius Cæsar, thou art mighty yet!"

is not a conclusion forced upon Brutus by the confusions and disasters of the battlefield, but the keynote of all that has happened before and after the assassination of the titular hero.

In the plays we have already studied, Hamlet, Richard III. and Macbeth admit us into the most secret chambers of their mind. We know their hopes and regrets, their ambitions and fears, the worst and the best of their nature; but Brutus resolutely closes his heart against us. We hear him *thinking* aloud, but that is a voluntary act. His inmost feeling he keeps to himself, save when for one instant only he lifts the veil and gives us a brief glimpse of what is going on within.

This is at the end of the soliloquy (II., 1.) in which he reasons with himself as to the necessity for Cæsar's death—reasoning which we see to be forced and in antagonism to his truer *instinct;* then he adds, with unusual self-revelation :—

" Since Cassius first did whet me against
        Cæsar
    I have not slept,
    Between the acting of a dreadful thing
    And the first motion, all the interim is
    Like a phantasma or a hideous dream :
    The *Genius* and the *mortal instruments*
    Are then in council, and the state of
        man,

76

Like to a little kingdom, suffers then
The nature of an insurrection."

Here we have again a reference to the
double nature of man. As with the
"Genius" of Macbeth (*Macb.*, III., 1.),
and the "Angel," "Demon," or "Spirit"
of Mark Antony (*Ant. and Cleo.*, II. 3.),
the "Genius" is here also spoken of as a
distinct part of the human being. Brutus
goes further, and defines for us the other
part of man as "the mortal instruments,"
in which is included, as can be gathered
from the context, the brain or reasoning
faculty. Throughout the play we can
trace, by the help of his own key, the
struggle going on within the breast of
Brutus. In the first act his "Genius"
is in revolt against the growing power of
Cæsar and the loss of Roman liberty.

77

Although his stoicism leads him to submit with dignity, he is "at war with himself," and feels that he would

> " Rather be a villager
> Than to repute myself a son of Rome
> Under these hard conditions as this
>   time
> Is like to lay upon us."

Cassius tries in vain to arouse in him jealousy of Cæsar or personal ambition, but an impassioned reference to his great ancestor, Junius Brutus of Tarquinian fame, excites his patriotic spirit, and the forged letters, purporting to be from the Roman citizens, and appealing to him for help, complete the conquest.

That is to say, his "mortal instruments" are won over to their faction, and his brain persuades itself that Cæsar must die, but now the "Genius" leans to the other side. It shrinks from a decision that involves perfidy to a friend, it protests against the disproportion of the punishment to the offence, for Cæsar, though an autocrat, was no tyrant, and it rises in revolt against the sanguinary disposition of the other conspirators.

It warns in vain; but when the irrevocable deed has been done, to be followed by all its tragic consequences, the outraged "Genius" of Brutus asserts itself ever more strongly, till, in the tent at Sardis, it stands fact to face with the "Genius," or the ghost of the murdered Cæsar.

The actual Cæsar who figures in the play is little of a hero, or more correctly, he is the wreck of one. Qualities good in themselves, but indulged in to excess, have lowered the tone of his character. What was once the self-confidence of conscious power has changed into vainglorious boasting. Appreciation of merited praise has degenerated into love of the grossest flattery. His noble pride has become insolent arrogance. If he had not been portrayed thus (and it is a development sanctioned more or less by historical facts), even Shakespeare's mighty genius could scarcely have won sympathy for his murderers.

But the memory of Cæsar *as he was* palpitates through the first three Acts of the play, and from the moment when the daggers of the assassins "hack each other in his sides," the sword of Brutus alone going straight and true to his heart, Cæsar's liberated spirit becomes the lead-ing influence of the tragedy, and even Brutus is subordinate to it.

Mark Antony's words indicate this :—

" Cæsar's spirit, ranging for revenge,
With Até by his side come hot from
  hell,
Shall in these confines with a monarch's voice
Cry, Havoc! and let slip the dogs of
  war."

The revengeful spirit seems already to pursue Brutus and Cassius as they ride "like madmen through the gates of Rome." It hovers over the city while the bloodthirsty mob tear his ill-omened name out of the poet Cinna's heart. It looks down with sad cynicism (or might do so) while Octavius, Antony, and Lepidus, to make room for whom he had been

F

slain, drew out the black list of the hundred senators (including Cicero) who are to die, and consult how they can best circumvent the generosity of his, the murdered Cæsar's, will. We trace its influence on the distracted Portia, when her noble intellect totters under the general crash, and her unendurable anxiety and grief are ended by her own despairing act.

And Brutus—was the accusing spirit ever absent from his mind?

" Remember March, the Ides of March
    remember !"

he said to Cassius. He himself never forgot. On that direful day he had struck for liberty, and the result was chaos.

The sudden outburst of wrath against the dishonesty of his foster-brother was but the climax of a storm that had been long gathering in his tormented soul:

"Did not great Julius bleed for justice sake?
What *villain* touched his body that did stab
And not for justice?"

Again his agony finds vent in scathing words, which, at the same time, betray the position still held in his mind by the dead—yet still living—Cæsar:

"What, shall one of us
That struck *the foremost man of all this world*
But for supporting robbers, shall we now
Contaminate our fingers with base bribes,

And sell the mighty space of our large
 honours
For so much trash as can be grasped
 thus?"

When the fruitless wrath had evapor-
ated into equally hopeless sadness,
Brutus, the Stoic philosopher, confesses
in the weakness that comes with re-
action :

"O Cassius, I am sick with many
 griefs!"

On the same night, after having re-
sisted Cassius' persuasion to protract this
state of civil war, and decided to hazard
all for one side or the other on the
morrow, he was left alone in his tent.
Alone—for although he had asked Varro
and Claudius to remain with him, his

courtesy would not permit them to "stand and watch" as they proposed to do, and they are now fast asleep on the floor.

He had asked for a song to ward off the thought that threatens to take possession of him, but slumber had "laid his leaden mace also on the boy that played him music," and he had gently removed the instrument that it might not be broken and the weary sleeper disturbed.

He tries to read, opening his book at the place which he had had marked, but that too fails him. The one persistent, unconquerable thought claims possession of his mind—the thought of the friend he had sacrificed in vain. At last, in the silence and solitude, accentuated rather than broken by the heavy breathing of the three sleepers, the influence that has been haunting his destiny resolves itself into form, and the Ghost of Cæsar stands before him :

"How ill this taper burns!   Ha! who
    comes here?
I think it is the weakness of mine eyes
That shapes this monstrous apparition.
It comes upon me.   Art thou any-
    thing?
Art thou some god, some angel, or
    some devil
That makest my blood cold and my
    hair to stand?
Speak to me, who thou art!"
GHOST: "Thy evil spirit, Brutus."

What a volume of meaning there is in the term.   Brutus makes no attempt to refute it, but, even while his blood runs cold in presence of the unearthly visitor, he asks as calmly as he had addressed Cæsar during life:

GHOSTS.

"Wherefore art thou come?"
GHOST: "To tell thee thou shalt see me
    at Philippi."
"Well," quietly answers the philosopher:
    "Then I shall see thee again?"
GHOST: "Ay, at Philippi."

And now Brutus understands and accepts the information that at Philippi he will meet his former friend, his present foe, on equal terms in the land of the hereafter.   He responds with increased interest:

"Why, I will see thee at Philippi then,"

and would fain ask more, but the Ghost had gone

BRUTUS: "Now I have taken heart, thou
    vanishest. Ill spirit, I would
    hold more talk with thee."

But it was in vain. The spirit might still be near, but Brutus had lost the power of seeing it. Filled with curiosity as well as awe, he turns his investigations in another direction.

BRUTUS: "Boy, Lucius! Varro! Claudius! Sirs, awake! Claudius!"

LUCIUS: "The strings, my lord are false."

BRUTUS: "He thinks he still is at his instrument. Lucius, awake!"

LUCIUS: "My lord!"

BRUTUS: "Didst thou dream, Lucius, that thou so criedst out?"

LUCIUS: "I did not know that I did cry, my lord."

BRUTUS: "Yes, that thou didst. Didst thou see anything?"

LUCIUS: "Nothing, my lord."

BRUTUS: "Sleep again, Lucius."

He addresses the same questions to the two soldiers, with the same result. The visit of the Evil Spirit had been for himself alone.

On the battlefield the Spirit was still present. Cassius was dimly conscious of it when he looked with unaccustomed misgiving at the choughs and crows that followed the devoted army; we feel too that it was no natural part of his character that made him "misconstrue everything," and, taking defeat for granted, precipitate it by falling on his own sword.

Brutus acknowledges its all-conquering presence when, on seeing the dead bodies of Cassius and Titinius, he exclaims :—

" O Julius Cæsar, thou art mighty yet.

> Thy spirit walks abroad, and turns our
> swords
> In our own proper entrails."

At one time during the fight, although the exact moment is not revealed, the Spirit once again became visible to the intensified soul of Brutus. There is no suggestion of illusion or hallucination in his quiet words to Voluminius:

> "The ghost of Cæsar hath appeared to
> me
> Two several times by night : at Sardis
> once,
> And this last night here in Philippi
> fields :
> I know my hour is come."

Death had not sought him on the field, therefore the Ghost's assignation was not merely prophetic. Brutus regarded the

second appearance as a command. He
had told Cassius, when bidding him farewell before the battle, that he found it

> " Cowardly and vile
> For fear of what might fall, so to
> prevent
> The time of life."

But now Cæsar's summons has convinced him that his time has come and
that he must be his own executioner. As
he falls upon the sword, which on the
fatal Ides of March had broken the harmony of his life, his last words are at
once a resolution of all its discords and
a fitting close to its tragic strain :

> " Cæsar, now be still :
> I killed not thee with half so good a
> will."

SUPERNATURAL IN SHAKESPEARE.

So, in this drama of two worlds, we leave the Ghost of Brutus as well as of Cæsar in the unseen world, while Octavius and Antony pursue their victorious earthly career, until they in turn oppose one another, and Octavius carries on the tradition of the mighty Julius alone.

It may be said that the spirits of Cæsar and of Brutus still contend in and over this "narrow world"; the former, with haughty insolence, arrogating power and wealth with the one hand, while doling out contemptuous charity with the other; the latter still beating against the wall, striking for liberty, agonising in defeat, baulked by the self-interest of associates, the fickleness of the mob, the want of practical wisdom on his own part, but approaching ever nearer and nearer to the goal when—not the proud, not the cunning, not the tyrant—but the just and wise and meek shall inherit and rule in the earth.

PART III.

—

FAIRIES.

Since when have fairies existed, and how did they come into being?

If we use the word in its widest sense, merely as representing imaginary forms without tangible existence, we must go back to the world's childhood to discover their genesis.

As long as there has been the darkness of night and the mystery of moonlight, the secret forest and the hidden waterfall, the mountain cave and the "dismal swamp," so long has the earth been peopled by the imagination with gods and devils, giants and dwarfs, hobgoblins and gnomes, genii and spirits.

These have been suggested partly no

94

doubt by the occasional monstrosities seen in life, but chiefly by the secret powers of nature and the qualities, good and bad, that exist in the hearts and influence the destinies of human beings.

But if we think of fairies in the modern sense as beautiful or grotesque little beings of human form, dancing on the green-sward and hiding in the flowers; or speeding through the air on some benevolent or, it may be, mischievous errand, the fairies of Hans Anderson, of Sir Noel Paton, of Mrs. S. C. Hall, then I am glad to have the authority of Charles Lamb for the statement that they are the creation of Shakespeare.

They were created perhaps not *entirely* out of nothing, but we seek in vain in English or Saxon mythology for any precursors of these exquisite embodiments of everything that is fanciful and fascinating.

"The fairies of folk-lore," if we may borrow the words and rest on the authority of Mr. Harry Furness, "were rough and repulsive, taking their style from the hempen home-spuns who invented them."

The pretended fairies in "The Merry Wives of Windsor" may be akin to them, but those of "A Midsummer Night's Dream" are of completely different race.

There are indeed suggestions in the mythology of the Bretons and in the Pantheon of the Gauls of the modern world of fancy, but the thought which gave birth to the "let there be" of Shake-

96

speare's fairy-land, had its origin in the nymphs and fauns, the naiads and dryads of Greece.

They had slumbered long, these exquisite inhabitants of the Athenian woods, resting within the covers of dingy volumes, wrapped in the crabbed letters of an unknown tongue, but at last they had been set free, with all their human contemporaries of classic fame, to preside over the birth and help in the development of our English drama.

How much Shakespeare owed to the spirit and the inspiration of the Greek writers we have learned at last from Dr. Collins' careful research.

But even these beautiful fancies were not *imitated* by our dramatist, but re-created by the magic of his genius, so

G

that our fairies, while indebted for their gracefulness and beauty to their Athenian ancestors, are purely and intensely English.

First in that inimitable kingdom, into which we are admitted as we study this most imaginative of all the immortal dramas, stands Titania, Queen of the Fairies.

When we remember her gentle grace and dignity, we are not surprised to learn that she can trace her pedigree back to the time before Jupiter reigned in Olympus, being, as her name implies, a daughter of the Titans.

It is even so. Titania can have no other meaning, and Ovid had already in his "Metamorphoses" invented the title, applying it to Diana, to Latona, and to

Circe in order to accentuate their descent from these ancient and powerful beings.

There was a translation by Golding of Ovid's Metamorphoses extant early enough to have been used by the dramatist, but in it the word "Titania" does not occur, although used four times by Ovid. Instead of adopting this name for Diana and the others, Golding paraphrases it as "daughter of the Titans" or other such expression. It was in the original Latin of Ovid, as Professor Baynes long ago pointed out, that Shakespeare found the name and made it for all time the cognomen of the Queen of the English Fairies.

It has always seemed to me an impertinence to associate the necessity for translations with the name of Shakespeare, as though the Genius who could not only create imaginative worlds but make the real past live again before us, who could not alone probe the secrets of the human heart, but reveal the mysteries of nature and open the windows of the Infinite, would be content to stand behind the closed door of an unknown tongue and be indebted to others for the treasures hidden within. Let us hope that the scholarly articles by Dr. Collins in the "Fortnightly Review," added to the Studies of Mr. Theobald and others, have, by proving the dramatist to have been a classical scholar, put an end for ever to this nightmare of Shakespearean criticism.

Of Titania's train of attendants four are introduced to us by titles which proclaim them to be the embodied spirits of Nature's loveliness.

There are also musicians to lull her to sleep, little elves to clothe whom the reremouse must yield his wings, one special warrior brave and strong enough to face the monster squirrel and rob him of his nuts, and, lastly, a little human changeling boy, much loved by Titania and the cause of strife between her and the King.

Oberon's descent is also royal, but not so ancient as that of Titania. He probably inherits his name and his realm from a certain Auberon who figures in the old French romance, "Huon of Bordeaux," and whose kingdom, like that of Shakespeare's Oberon, was eastward from Jerusalem, somewhere in that mysterious land, known at that time by the vague generic name of India.

This Auberon was the reputed son of Julius Cæsar and his mother was no less a person than Morgan le Fay, the British King Arthur's sister.

In every other respect the Auberon of the French tale is a completely different conception, the character of Shakespeare's Oberon being as original as it is beautiful. His fairy followers are probably more or less similar to those of Titania, but his henchman and familiar spirit deserves special notice.

Puck alone is thoroughly English and is well-known in folk-lore under the name of Robin Goodfellow. If we trace his pedigree further still, we are carried northward to the Icelandic Puki, the "wee devil" of the Norseman. He may even bear some relation to the Pouke of "Piers the Ploughman," which also has a Satanic meaning, but if so, he is a very purified little devil, with no greater sin than love of a prank and a preference for seeing things "befall preposterously."

In this dream of a Midsummer Night the first and last Acts (with the exception of one short episode) take place in the palace of Theseus. The three intermediate Acts have for their scene "a wood near Athens."

In the palace the human element is supreme, human reasoning, human laws prevail; but the moment we enter the wood we feel that we are on enchanted ground—the forest, for the time being, has become fairy-land.

From diverse sides Oberon and Titania, with their attendants, are slowly approaching. We can almost hear the twittering of the tiny wings, and the rhythmic motion of the King and Queen as they move through the leafy glades lit up with mystic moonlight, while their little heralds "Puck" and "a fairy" appear first upon the scene.

In this wonderful realm even old Father Time has to lay down his hour-glass and cease to be a tyrant. Of the four tedious days that have to elapse in the human sphere before Theseus can claim Hippolyta as his bride, here three of them are merged into one single night; while on the other hand, of one short minute which would to Theseus' courtiers seem an inconsiderable portion of time, one-third is enough for the fairy followers of Titania to kill the canker in the musk-rose-buds and to war with the rere-mice for their leathern wings.

The moon is equally subservient, for we are told circumstantially by Theseus in the opening of the play that there will be a new moon on his wedding night, four days hence, therefore, according to Nature's routine, there could be but a faint streak visible for one or two hours before sunrise.

But the clowns, after consulting a calendar (found presumably in the wood) are informed by Quince that there will be moonshine on the night of the revels. This, indeed, can scarcely be adduced as evidence on one side or the other, since Peter Quince, honest soul, might naturally suppose that a new moon, like other new things, would shine with special brilliance.

We find, however, that Oberon's first greeting to the Queen is:

"Ill met by moon-light, proud Titania!" (II. 1.) and she, in her turn, invites him (on condition of good behaviour) to join their moon-light revels.

But when, in the last Act, we return to the palace of Theseus, there is no more question of the moon, or of opening the casement to admit its beams; Nature calmly resumes her sway, and a bush and lantern have to do duty for the non-existent moonshine.

We are reminded vividly by Titania of our indebtedness to the fairies when she describes the disastrous effect upon the

weather by the cessation of their revels,
which have been rudely disturbed by
Oberon's "brawls"—his jealous efforts
to obtain possession of the changeling.

Even the solid framework of the earth
gives way under their gentle but irresis-
tible power, when the reconciled royalties
join hands and gently

"Rock the ground whereon these
mortals sleep."

In this land of enchantment and ethereal
beauty, the rustic clowns, and even the
Athenian lovers as they blunder through
the scene, seem but clumsy interlopers;
their judgment, their affections, their
movements, their very appearance, all are
subject to the whims of the fairies and we
feel almost contemptuously that they

serve a sufficiently high purpose in making sport for the irrepressible Puck.

"Lord, what fools these mortals be!"

exclaims the tricksy spirit with the insight of long experience.

Oberon takes the matter seriously. He has come from the farthest steppe of India to bless with joy and prosperity the nuptials of Hippolyta and Theseus and he feels keen sympathy with the two other pairs of human lovers.

But his first task is to overcome the determination of Titania to retain in her own service the "lovely boy stolen from an Indian King."

"Why should Titania cross her Oberon?" he asks, coaxingly. "I do but beg a little changeling boy to be my henchman."

But she answers loftily :

"Set your mind at rest.
The fairy-land buys not the boy of me.
His mother was a vot'ress of my order :
And, in the spiced Indian air by night,
Full often hath she gossiped by my
    side,
And sat with me by Neptune's yellow
    sands.

. . . . .

But she, being mortal, of that boy did
    die,
And for her sake I do rear up her boy,
And for her sake I will not part with
    him."—(II. 1.).

And so once more they part in anger,
the Queen withdrawing with her train,

and Oberon remaining to consult with
Puck.

Alas, poor Titania! What chance
has she, with all her royal dignity,
against the knowledge and craft of her
lord and his clever little attendant spirit?

Ere long Puck is speeding away, so
swiftly that he could "put a girdle round
the earth in forty minutes," to a little
western isle where once Cupid had aimed
his dart

" At a fair vestal throned in the west."

It had been labour wasted, for the fiery
dart was

" Quenched in the chaste beams of the
    watery moon
And the imperial vot'ress passed on
In maiden meditation, fancy free."
(II., 1.).

FAIRIES.

But the arrow which had missed the heart of the Maiden Queen pierced a little milk-white flower which straight turned purple with the wound.

This flower Oberon must needs have, for its juice, squeezed upon the eyelids of the hapless Titania while asleep, will make her

                      " madly dote
Upon the next live creature that she sees.

. . . .

Be it a lion, bear, or wolf, or bull,
Or meddling monkey or on busy ape.
She shall pursue it with the soul of
    love :
And ere I take this charm from off her
    sight,
As I can take it with another herb,
I'll make her render up her page to
    me."—(II., 1.).

SUPERNATURAL IN SHAKESPEARE.

When Puck returns Oberon knows well where to seek the alienated Queen, and we too know that lovely bank with its soft and fragrant bed of wild thyme and oxslips and nodding violets, and its canopy of luscious woodbine, sweet musk-roses and eglantine. There sleeps Titania; and there by the combined malice of her lord and the mischievous prank of Puck she awakes to see and to love the transformed weaver—Bottom with the ass' head.

Let us draw a veil over the humiliating scene.

But even through this ordeal Titania passes without loss of feminine charm or royal dignity. Her homely swain's jest on the estrangement between love and

reason draws from her the earnest assur-
ance :

"Thou art as wise as thou art beautiful,"

a compliment which even Bottom's
vanity cannot accept without a protest.
" Nay, not so, neither," he ejaculates.

   She appoints four elves, name-children
of the delicate pea-blossom, the dew be-
spangled cobweb, the feathery, flutter-
ing moth, the sharp, though diminutive,
mustard-seed to attend to his wishes; and
when the coarse mortal, reminded by
their dainty names only of the pleasures
of the palate, prates on about pease
squash and roast beef, she issues the
gentle command

" Tie up my love's tongue : bring him
   silently."—(III., 1.).

113

H

Titania is not the first, nor will she be the last, to lavish a wealth of tender affection upon coarse sensuality. And yet Bottom is not all worthless—in the eyes of his fellows at least he is the properest handicraftsman in all Athens to play the lover before the duke, and apparently the most popular.

The memory of that visit to fairy-land will remain with him to the end of his life, vivid, but unutterable.

"I have had a most rare vision," he stammers as he wakes out of his enchanted sleep; "I have had a dream. Methought I was—there is no man can tell what. Methought I was—and methought I had—but man is but a patched fool if he will offer to say what methought I had."—(IV., 1.).

When he rejoins his comrades he exclaims :—

" Masters I am to discourse wonders :
but ask me not what."

Is it some half conscious effect of the
dainty vision that makes him say so
emphatically in his instructions to the
performers :

" In any case let Thisby have clean
linen !"

There seems to be a certain elevation in
all his later remarks, culminating in the
final half symbolic statement, reminding
us of the last scene in "Romeo and
Juliet" :

" No, I assure you, the wall is down that
divided their fathers."

Farewell, sweet bully Bottom. The ass' head may have been but a visible symbol of what already existed, but there is a heart beneath thy home-spun garments and thy immortal soul has not been altogether dead to the ethereal vision.

How different was it with Titania when her lord, pitying at last her dotage, and having won his point about the little Indian boy, removes the charm from her eyes, and counteracts with Dian's bud the effect of "Cupid's flower."

She finds no difficulty in expressing the sordid truth of her dream.

"I dreamt I was enamoured of an ass!" Adding, as her eye falls upon the still sleeping form of the weaver:

"Oh, how mine eyes do loathe his visage
  now!"

Disillusion swift and complete—an experience to be driven shudderingly from
the little fairy brain.

And now all is harmony again in fairy-
land. The wood is filled with delicate
music in sweetest accord with the rustle
of the leaves and the purling of the
brook: the five human sleepers are
rocked as in a cradle into deeper slumber;
the deforming head is removed from the
unfortunate rustic; by means of the
potent juice Lysander is restored to
Hermia, and Demetrius made to return
Helena's love. Happy in the result of
his long night's work Oberon addresses
Titania:

" Thou and I are new in amity;
And will to-morrow midnight solemnly
Dance in Duke Theseus' house
    triumphantly,
And bless it to all fair prosperity."

But there have been repeated warnings
that dawn is approaching.   Puck had already warned his master :

" My fairy lord, this must be done in
    haste,
    For night's swift dragons cut the
      clouds full fast
    And yonder shines Aurora's har-
      binger !
    At whose approach ghosts wandering
      here and there
    Troop home to churchyards : damned
      spirits all,
    That in cross ways and floods have
      burial,
    Already to their wormy beds have gone

For fear lest day should look their
  shames upon;
They wilfully themselves exile from
  light,
And must for aye consort with black-
  browed night."

This speech of Puck's gives us fresh
insight into Ghost-lore, revealing that it
is by no inexorable law that wandering
spirits dread the "bird of dawning," but
the result of their own guilty consciousness and shame.   Should a blessed spirit
vouchsafe to visit the scene of his earthly
career he would, we are led to suppose,
be as much at ease by daylight as by
dark.

  Oberon makes haste to dissociate himself from the unhappy ghosts, exclaiming :—

" But we are spirits of another sort :
  I with the Morning's love have oft
    made sport :
  And, like a forrester, the grove may
    tread,
  Even till the Eastern gate, all fiery red,
  Opening for Neptune with fair blessed
    beams,
  Turns into yellow gold his salt green
    streams,
  But, notwithstanding haste, make no
    delay,
  We may effect this business yet ere
    day."—(III., 2.).

Now the business has been effected and
the faithful attendant once more sounds
the warning :

PUCK : "Fairy King, attend and mark
           I do hear the morning lark."
OBERON : "Then my Queen in silence
              sad

FAIRIES.

Trip we after the night's shade:
We the globe can compass soon
Swifter than the wandering moon."
(IV., 1.).

The Fairies are gone—the wood has become an ordinary sunlit forest—the sound of wind-horns drives away the last breath of enchantment. The hunters come upon the scene, the sleepers awake and after confused explanations the three happy couples with the perforce consenting Egeus wend their way to the temple and the feast.

When the wedding rites are over and the first night of revels has been brought to a close by the performance of "Pyramus" and his cronies, when all have been dismissed by the noble Theseus to whom
" Never anything can be amiss
When simpleness and duty tender it.";

when the palace is silent and the indwellers sunk in repose, once more the fairies float into our view, the King and Queen in their grace and beauty, the lovely little elves with song and dance and Puck as ever in the van.

The merry spirit opens the scene with lines which Coleridge pronounced to be pure Anacreon in perfectness, proportion, grace, and spontaneity :

PUCK : "Now the hungry lion roars,
    And the wolf behowls the moon;
    Whilst the heavy ploughman snores,
    All with weary task foredone.
    Now the wasted brands do glow,
    Whilst the screech-owl, screeching
        loud,
    Puts the wretch that lies in woe,
    In remembrance of a shrowd.

FAIRIES.

Now it is the time of night,
That the graves all gaping wide
Every one lets forth his sprite
In the church-way path to glide:
And we fairies that do run
By the triple Hecate's team,
From the presence of the sun
Following darkness like a dream,
Now are frolic; not a mouse
Shall disturb this hallowed house:
I am sent with broom before
To sweep the dust behind the door."
(V., 2.).

The magic broom having done its duty, the royal pair, with their iridescent train of spirits enter the building and Oberon issues his fairy commands:

OBERON: "Through the house give
shimmering light
By the dead and drowsy fire;
Every elf and fairy sprite

Hop as light as bird from brier
And this ditty after me
Sing and dance it trippingly."

Titania also gives final directions to her tiny followers ere the great ceremony begins.

TITANIA : "First rehearse your song by
    rote,
To each word a warbling note.
Hand in hand, with fairy grace,
Will we sing and bless this place."

They come now as visitors. Their presence does not transform the human-built dwelling into fairyland, but as the ethereal and gracious beings pass from room to room

" And each several chamber bless
  Through the palace with sweet peace,"

we realise something of the unseen influences that control and guide our mortal
lives, shaping to a perfect issue our
rough-hewn designs.

In this play, as in so many other cases,
Shakespeare explains his own position.

When Hermia and Helena and their
respective lovers have fully described all
they can remember of the wondrous night
spent in the wood, Hippolyta and
Theseus discuss together the marvels they
have heard.

Theseus is incredulous and declares
that

" The lunatic, the lover and the poet
    Are of imagination all compact;
    One sees more devils that vast hell can
        hold,
    That is, the madman : the lover, all as
        frantic,

Sees Helen's beauty in a brow of
Egypt;
The poet's eye in a fine frenzy rolling,
Doth glance from heaven to earth, from
earth to heaven,
And as imagination bodies forth
The forms of things unknown, the
poet's pen
Turns them to shapes, and gives to
airy nothing
A local habitation and a name.
Such tricks hath strong imagination,"
&c.

Hippolyta replies :

"But all the story of the night told over,
And all their minds transfigured so
together
More witnesseth than fancy's images,
And grows to something of great
constancy."—(V., 1.).

And she is right; for it is the "sweet

reasonableness" of "The Dream" that appeals to us most strongly.

The harmony is so perfect between the poet's graceful fancies and the sights and sounds of Nature in her softest aspect, that uncompromising disbelief in it all would carry us further from the inner truth of things than even child-like credulity.

Who, even if he have not himself suffered from the poison, does not know the effect of Cupid's magic flower, making maidens see a Hyperion where we behold a Satyr, or a youth read the smile of an angel in the wanton grimaces of a Circe. Who has not longed for the power of Oberon to anoint their eyes with the Dian's bud of reason, knowing too well that human interference will only intensify the poison?

We know, too, that the boasted speed of Puck was no ignorant fancy, but a prophetic intuition grounded on knowledge as thorough as was then attainable.

It may indeed be doubted whether any embodiment of imagination, or even of faith, can be of real and lasting value to humanity, unless the ladder of reason and knowledge has first been laboriously scaled to the topmost round, and the flight of thought continued from that lofty height. The intuitions and inventions of an untaught genius may be interesting as a study, but they could never evoke a response from every shade of human character, and from every nationality as Shakespeare's words have done.

128

FAIRIES.

A still more perfect example of imagination continued along the lines of knowledge and reason is to be found in "The Tempest," to which we now turn as a final example of the Supernatural in the Shakespeare plays.   There is a certain resemblance between the earlier and later Fairy Dramas, but Shakespeare had to study much, think much, suffer much before the fairy King Oberon and his merry henchman Puck could be developed into Prospero, the lord of Nature, and Ariel his faithful slave.

PART IV.

—

SPRITES, &c.

" The Tempest" was one of the last, if not the last, play that Shakespeare wrote, and yet, when in 1623 the first complete edition of the works appeared, it was placed in the forefront of the volume.

When we regard this drama as a whole, it does indeed form a suitable prologue to the great poetical masterpieces. It seems to epitomize the life work of the dramatist. It symbolises the malevolent powers against which he had waged war and the beneficent secrets of Nature over which he had gained the mastery. It places the poet before us in the attitude of one who "stands upon the vantage ground of truth, and sees the errors and wanderings and mists and tempests in the vale below, but with pity, and not with swelling or pride."—(*Essay of Truth*, Bacon).

From the beginning of his dramatic career Shakespeare proclaims his hatred of ignorance and his reverence for knowledge—that is for true knowledge as opposed to mere learning.

Already in "Love's Labour Lost," a work of his youth, he tells us that

" Study is like the heaven's glorious sun,
    That will not be deep searched with
      saucy looks
    Small have continual plodders ever won
    Save base authority from others'
      books."—(I., 1.).

That this is not the mere prejudice of

131

an unlearned man is proved by the following words of the King of Navarre:

" How well he's read to reason against
   reading !"

Hamlet, Horatio, Bassanio, Brutus,
Proteus, Posthumus were all scholars.
Indeed, unless it be Othello, who, nevertheless, was master of his own profession,
our full sympathy is never demanded for
any unlearned man. The unsophisti-
cated genius, the self-made dignitary, are
entirely absent from the dramatis personæ
of Shakespeare's plays.

To teach and to elevate the human race
had been the object of "that great heart
of his," as well as to "adorn the age in
which he lived" with the most marvellous
creations of the imagination built upon

the solid foundation of truth that the world has ever seen.

"There is no darkness but ignorance," the clown, masquerading as priest, tells Malvolio (*Twelfth Night*, IV., 2.); and the position is summed up in the words of Lord Say to the bloodthirsty men of Kent:

" Seeing that ignorance is the curse of God
And knowledge the wing wherewith we fly to heaven,
Unless ye be possessed with devilish spirits,
Ye cannot but forbear to murder me."

But Shakespeare learned before his pen was laid down for ever that there is something darker and viler than simple, nay, even than brutal ignorance.

133

SUPERNATURAL IN SHAKESPEARE.

To have every opportunity of receiving the light and yet to prefer darkness; to have knowledge but to employ it only for base self-gratification; to have power, but to use it for cursing not blessing; to be endowed with the dual human nature, a union of the animal with the divine, and to use the divine light of reason to intensify the animal; it is of such it seems to me, not of the low savage, or the mere sensualist, or the ignorant criminal that Caliban is the symbol—he is not earthy but devilish.

It may safely be said, a circumstance unique in the Shakespeare plays, that Caliban is not meant to be sympathised with in any one particular.

It is true that he had been his own king, and lord of the island before the advent of Prospero, but had he been a willing disciple, he might, under his tuition, have become infinitely more a lord and a king over Nature and himself. His inheritance had been a terrible one, being the offspring of the devil and the witch Sycorax (I., 2.), but even this does not free him from responsibility.

It would be difficult perhaps to recognise in the highly respectable Pharisees of Scripture, the Caliban of "The Tempest," and yet the stern words were addressed to them, "Ye are of your father, the devil."

Had Caliban made the slightest effort to respond to the claims of truth and beauty when presented to him, the benevolence of Prospero and the tender pity

of Miranda would have helped him to
overcome the disabilities of heredity.

> "Abhorred slave,
> Which any print of goodness *wilt* not
> take
> Being capable of all ill."

As the seal is to the impression, so is
truth to goodness, we are told by the
great Elizabethan philosopher. — (See
Adv. of Learning, 1st Book, VIII., 2.).

But the seal of truth had failed to make
any impression of goodness on Caliban's
will, susceptible as he was to every evil
influence.

It is noteworthy that his mother, the
foul witch Sycorax, was not utterly vile.
When banished from Argier, "For one
thing she did they would not take her

life."—(I. 2.). But in Caliban there is
no redeeming quality. Prospero ex-
pressly states that he "did learn," but
when the opportunity comes he uses what
knowledge he has in an attempt to murder
his benefactor. He was able to express
himself in powerful and even poetical
language, but he himself declares :

" You taught me language and my profit
    on't
  Is, I know how to curse."

He was open to the power of beauty—
(III. 2.), but he would have degraded it
to the very dust. He could appreciate
music, distinguish the right tune from
the wrong, and describe the varied
sounds of the island in almost ravishing
words, but its only effect upon him was

137

to lull his energies to sleep and make him dream of "riches ready to drop on him."

Caliban was religious—in a sense. He must always have a deity and he attributes each event of his life to that influence. If he falls in the mire or wanders from the path, if he stumbles over a hedgehog, is tormented by apes, or bitten by adders, it is because Prospero has willed it. If he escapes calamity, it is because the spirits have not been bidden to molest him.

It is the religion of fear. He grudgingly obeys Prospero because his power is such that he could control even his "dam's god, Setebos."

But when Stephano comes with his magic liquor and his swaggering air, and

138

tells him that he has come from the moon, Caliban at once transfers his allegiance and is willing to grovel at his feet. With such a god what would not he be capable of?

"Beat him enough," he cries, as Trinculo shrinks from his comrade's blows; "after a little time I'll beat him too," that is, when he has been made helpless and utterly unable to retaliate.

He offers to lead the two drunkards to the tent where (like Hamlet's father) it is Prospero's custom to sleep in the afternoon.

> "There thou mayst brain him
> . . . . or with a log
> Batter his skull, or paunch him with
> a stake
> Or cut his wezand with thy knife."

139

Nothing is too cruel if only he can rid himself of him whom he calls his tyrant.

The history of Caliban seems to forbid the thought that he is meant to represent the savage, the cannibal, or the mere earth-spirit. His mother was not ignorant, but on the contrary possessed magic powers, and, although she could not command him, she had skill to torment and render helpless the delicate spirit Ariel.

She had been banished from Argier, the seat at one time of civilization, at another of piracy, but never within historic times of savagery or cannibalism. Her name is most probably derived from two Greek words, Sus (sow) and Korax (raven)—the typical sow, that was washed but returned to her "wallowing in the mire," and the raven of contemporary

140

reference : "To make the cause of religion to descend to the cruel and execrable actions of murthering princes, butchery of people, etc., is to bring down the Holy Ghost, instead of in the likeness of a dove, in the shape of a vulture or *raven.*" Sycorax, we are told, had used her power for "mischiefs manifold and services (too) terrible to enter human hearing."

It is therefore of witchcraft and sin, not of earth and ignorance, that Caliban is offspring. He may be considered the symbol of all the foul crimes committed against light and knowledge since the world began.

Hence his superiority to the mere drunkards, Trinculo and Stephano. Their vulgar utterances are invariably clothed in prose, but Caliban as invariably speaks in blank verse. They blunder along without any definite object, but Caliban is cunning and wary. They are diverted from the thought of the greater crime by the fine garments hung out as a lure, but Caliban never swerves from his purpose.

> " The dropsy drown this fool! what do
> you mean
> To dote thus on such luggage;"

and again :

> "I'll have none on't, we shall lose our
> time,
> And all be turned to barnacles or apes
> *With foreheads villainous low."*
> —(IV. 1.).

Even in his foul deformity he seems to dread the deterioration of intellect.

Prospero speaking, as it were, from the ultimate standpoint, sums up his opinion of the Calibans of the world in three sentences:

"As 'tis
We cannot miss him: he does make our
    fire,
Fetch in our wood and serve in offices
That profit us."

In other words, he will not help on the cause of truth, therefore he must serve those who will.

Secondly, as he will do no good, he must be so controlled that he can work no harm:

"Therefore wast thou
Deservedly confined into this rock
Who hadst deserved more than a
    prison."

143

Thirdly, and this Prospero admits with the deepest pain, he is hopeless :

" A devil, a born devil, on whose nature
　Nurture can never stick; on whom my
　　pains,
　Humanely taken, all, all lost, quite
　　lost;
　And as with age his body uglier grows,
　So his mind cankers."

Caliban's body grows by accretion as the ages pass on, and the outward monstrosity is symbolic of the mind within. There is one word, and one word only, in the play that suggests the possibility of hope for Caliban.

In the last scene when Prospero issues his final command :

"Go, sirrah, to my cell,
Take with you your companions; as
    you look
To have my pardon, trim it hand-
    somely,"

he answers:

"Ay, that I will, and I'll be wise here-
    after
And seek for *grace*."

Then he adds:

    "What a thrice double ass
Was I to take this drunkard for a god
And worship this dull fool,"

and we feel that only the certainty of
security would be needed to make him
turn once more against his benefactor.

Still, the very mention of the word
"grace" reminds us that when sin has

145

been driven from its last refuge, infinite love remains the same, and that

> " He that might the vantage best have took
> Found out the remedy."
> —(*Meas. for Meas*. II. 2.).

The exact antithesis to Caliban is not Ariel, but Prospero. In him we see man fully developed, with legitimate power over Nature and in complete sympathy with the divine Author.

His character is a combination of wisdom, knowledge, and goodness. His name suggests the high truth that in the end, however distant that end may be, prosperity is the inevitable result of such a combination. He is represented as one who, having been "led by nature in in-

146

vention is able to control her in action."
—(See Bacon in *Praise of Knowledge.*)

When we consider the wonderful advance made in this direction since the days of Shakespeare, during whose life-time utilitarian science received its first impulse, it is difficult to form any conception of what man may have achieved when three more centuries shall have passed away.

To utilize the lightning, to make the strong-based promontory shake, to reproduce voices, and in many ways to annihilate space, we already know to be within human possibility, and Prospero's power over the winds and the waves, and "all the qualities of the isle," merely anticipate still higher possibilities.

And yet this interpretation does not

quite account for Prospero. There is something more in the magician who puts on and off his magic robe at pleasure, who can summon the goddesses Juno, Ceres, and Iris from Olympas, who can make banquets appear and disappear, and who can venture to assert:

" Graves at my command
  Have waked their sleepers, oped, and
    let them forth
  By my so potent art."

He is not only the seer who from his Pisgan height can view the promised land, but the Dramatic Genius who, by his magic art, can create worlds of his own, and command, not alone the spirits of .Nature, but also the souls of men.

We can hardly claim as supernatural

148

Prospero's exquisite child, "The most admired Miranda," and yet she seems less a lovely maiden than the very type itself of maidenhood, free from every taint of earth, fresh as it presented itself first in the great Artist's mind.

Is it possible that she and Sycorax are of the same sex?

Caliban brings them into sharp contrast:

" I never saw a woman
  But only Sycorax, my dam, and she,
  But she as far surpasseth Sycorax
  As great'st does least."

They stand at the opposite ends of the scale of womanhood, and in the other plays, if we sought carefully, might be found every degree between.

And who and what is Ariel—that deli-

cate, quaint, dainty, tricksy spirit whose
name and nature have a charm all their
own, suggesting interpretations that
elude us even while we seem to grasp
them ?

His name suggests the atmosphere and
Prospero calls him "but air," but this is
too limited, and can only refer to his
impalpable form. He cannot be air alone
since he can flame and flash around King
Alphonso's ship. He cannot be fire, for
he can swim and tread the ooze of the
salt deep; nor, though he rides on the
curl'd clouds, can he be water, even in
its evanescent form, since he can with
impunity dive into fire.

Even the lightning does not fulfil all
the manifold requirements of his many-
sided nature. Had the play been written

in the nineteenth, instead of the seven-
teenth, century we might, it is true, have
thought of him as symbolic of electricity.
But although this fierce fluid may indeed
enter into the combination, Ariel is too
gentle to be explained by it alone.

He assumes the form of a sweet voiced
water nymph to draw Prince Ferdinand
towards Miranda, and that of a threaten-
ing harpy to terrify and madden the
"three men of sin."—(III., 3.).

He is chief of all the spirits of the isle
and the elves of hills, brooks, standing
lakes, and groves whom Prospero apos-
trophizes in his beautiful farewell to his
island home (V., 1.)

"By whose aid,
Weak masters though ye be, I have be-
dimmed

151

The noontide sun, called forth the mutin-
ous winds,
And 'twixt the green sea and the azured
vault,
Set roaring war: to the dread rattling
thunder
Have I given fire, and rifted Jove's stout
oak
With his own bolt: the strong-based
promontory
Have I made shake; and by the spurs
plucked up
The pine and cedar."

In all these potent spells, as well as
in the gentler offices, the "fine spirit"
was prime actor.

Taking into consideration these varied
qualities, Ariel would seem to be the
quintessence of the higher laws of Nature,
those forces which, invisible yet irresis-
tible, work in all material things. He is

152

the antithesis of the coarse magic used
by Sycorax. She also found her power
in Nature's secrets, but her charms were
loathsome poisons, wicked dew brushed
with raven's feathers from unwholesome
fen, bats, beetles, toads, all products
of darkness and slime. She was even
able to control Ariel, though she could
not bend him to her uses, and so he,
the spirit of light and liberty, was confined within a cloven pine, till Prospero
arrived, and with his art "made gape
the pine and let him out."

But Ariel, although freed from the
tyranny of sorcery and witchcraft, was not
yet to be perfectly free. In his constant
longing for liberty and Prospero's repeated promise that he shall be free, we
are reminded of the well known tendency

153

of all the elements and forces of Nature to escape, unless held prisoner by the ingenuity of man.

Ariel was a faithful and absolutely trustworthy servant to Prospero; he told him no lies, made no mistakings, served without grudge or grumbling; and, although he rejoices with all the joy of his being when at last he is relegated "to the elements," there was sympathy, if we cannot call it love, between him and his noble master.

Caliban's statement: "They" (the spirits), "all do hate him as rootedly as I," is utterly false.

He takes for granted that where there is service there must be hate, but Ariel is "a spirit of another sort."—(*M.N.D.* III., 2.)

"All hail, great master, grave sir, hail,
   I come
To answer thy best pleasure,"

are the first words we hear him utter.
Again, when Prospero welcomes him
with the words :

"Come with a thought! I thank thee,
Ariel : come,"

he replies :

"Thy thoughts I cleave to."

And in Act IV., I, 31, he asks with quaint
pathos :

"Do you love me, master?   No?"

while Prosper answers, "Dearly."   Nay,
more; Ariel sympathises, to a certain

155

extent, with his master also in his bene-
ficence, and on one occasion gently reminds him that "the rarer action is in
virtue than in vengeance."

He has obeyed Prospero in bringing
confusion and madness upon his enemies,
then, after describing the results of his
labours, he adds :

" Your charm so strongly works 'em
  That if you now beheld them, your
    affection
  Would become tender."
PROS : "Dost thou think so?"
ARIEL : "Mine would, sir, were I
    human."
PROS : "And mine shall.
  Hast thou, which art but air, a touch,
    a feeling
  Of their afflictions, and shall not myself
  One of their kind, that relish all as
    sharply

156

Passion as they, be kindlier moved
than thou art?"

The harmony is true and subtle
between the laws of Nature and "Nature's
monarch man"; those laws which,
emanating from the Creator, partake unconsciously of His character, and, when
rightly understood and employed, serve
to link the human intellect with the divine.

It is an interesting fact, and has been
pointed out by various writers, that the
name of Ariel occurs several times in
Isaiah XXIX., 1—7, and it may well be
that Shakespeare took the designation
and some of the characteristics of his delicate yet powerful spirit from this source.

The following words from the seventh
verse are of peculiar interest: "And the
multitudes of all the nations that fight

157

against Ariel. . . . . Shall be as a
dream of a night vision.''

" The cloud-capped towers, the gorgeous
    palaces,
The solemn temples, the great globe
    itself,
Yea, all which it inherit, shall dissolve
And, like this insubstantial pageant
    faded
Leave not a rack behind."—(IV., 1.).

To fight *with* Ariel, as Prospero proved,
is to be sure of victory.

In "The Tempest" we find the culmin-
ation of Shakespeare's treatment of the
Supernatural element in life. Dreams,
prophecies, presentiments, disembodied
spirits, secret influences, Nature's forces,
all are parts of one great scheme. The
known material world moves on side by

side with the unknown and spiritual, and, if the name of God is seldom on lips meant for the public stage, the whole trend of the plays is to reveal Him.

This may account for the anomaly that, while some commentators are still asking the question : "Was Shakespeare a Christian ?" others, with deeper insight, assert that in moral force and inspiration, the works of Shakespeare are second only to the Evangile itself.

THE END.

Ellis Limited, Printers, 137 Cheapside, and at Southend-on-Sea.

Printed in the United States
98520LV00002B/121-123/A

9 780548 113844